GETTING IT RIGHT

Freezer To Microwave Cooking

Edited by
Wendy Hobson

GW00359473

foulsham
London · New York · Toronto · Sydney

foulsham
Yeovil Road, Slough, Berkshire, SL1 4JH

ISBN 0-572-01885-1

Printed in Great Britain
at St. Edmundsburry Press, Bury St. Edmunds

CONTENTS

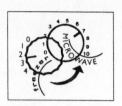

INTRODUCTION

The freezer and the microwave can work together in the kitchen as a real partnership, saving you time, energy and money, as well as helping you to create an interesting and varied, balanced diet for yourself and your family.

When you cook – either in the microwave or in the conventional oven – you can make larger quantities ready for the freezer. You can buy meat in bulk, or buy extra when it is reduced in the supermarket. You need never waste fruits and vegetables when they are plentiful and inexpensive – you can even pick your own for added economy.

Preparing for guests or parties becomes so much simpler as you can plan your cooking over several days or even weeks, making the most of times when you are less busy. And for those unexpected guests, there can always be something which can quickly be turned into a tasty snack, a delicious supper or even a family dinner.

The microwave defrosts food rapidly so there is no problem if you have forgotten to remove your evening meal from the freezer. Without a microwave, foods have to be defrosted for several hours so it is no good rushing to the freezer for a last minute dish.

For busy families and working people, the microwave and freezer make a wonderful team. Shopping can be done in bulk, food preparation can be fitted into weekends and evenings, and you can save time at the end of an exhausting day and still have a tasty meal.

With a little thought and planning, you can easily get into the habit of making the most of your microwave and freezer partnership. This book aims to give you all the basic facts you need to help you use them to the best advantage.

YOUR MICROWAVE OVEN

In the same way that you have to get to know your conventional oven, you need to get used to your microwave oven, for they do vary, in output, speed of cooking and so on. All it requires is a little practice, and you will soon acquire this as you experiment with the recipes in this book.

MICROWAVE OVENS

The majority of microwave ovens have a 600 watt output, although some older models are 500 watt and some are 700 watt. Most have a turntable on which the food revolves while cooking to maximise evenness of cooking. You still need to stir or rearrange foods during cooking, however. All microwave ovens have a timer and a number of levels of cooking, usually including a defrost facility.

Some ovens have automatic defrost or cooking facilities which save you working out how long to cook certain foods. These can be useful but are certainly not essential as you will soon become used to the cooking times you prefer for particular types of food.

Some microwave ovens have a browning element which can be used to brown foods before or after cooking.

Temperature sensors which control the cooking by the internal temperature of the food are available on some models.

Memory controls on some ovens mean that you can pre-set cooking times and levels in advance.

SUITABLE CONTAINERS

Check that the containers you use are suitable for the microwave. Pyrex, ceramic and many quality plastics are all suitable. Metal should never be used. Plastic should not be used for foods with a high fat or sugar content as they become too hot.

The shape of containers makes a difference to the way food cooks in a microwave oven. Large, round, shallow dishes are most suitable as the food cooks evenly and quickly. Square-cornered containers cause the food to overcook in the corners unless the food is regularly stirred. For foods with a high liquid content, use very large containers to allow for the liquid to rise up during cooking. Never use tall, narrow containers as the food inside can heat unevenly and may then splatter hot liquid out of the top.

To check whether a container is suitable, pour a cup of water into the container and microwave on high for 2 minutes. If the water is warm and the container cool, it is suitable. If the container is slightly warm, it can be used but food will take longer to cook. If the container is hot, it is not suitable.

ARRANGING FOOD IN THE CONTAINERS

Arrange uneven-shaped foods with the densest parts to the outside. Stir or rearrange foods regularly during cooking to ensure that the microwaves are penetrating throughout the food.

TIMING

Since cooking times are short, a small alteration can spoil the food. Always underestimate times as you can return food to the oven if necessary.

If you have a 500 watt oven, increase cooking times in the recipes by about 25 seconds per minute.

If you have a 700 watt oven, decrease cooking times in the recipes by about 25 seconds per minute.

STANDING TIMES

Foods will continue to defrost or cook after they have been removed from the microwave oven. Remember to allow for this in your timing, especially for cakes and similar items.

CLEANING YOUR MICROWAVE

Simply wipe your microwave clean after cooking with a damp cloth; never use abrasive cleaners. If food smells linger, boil a bowl of water with a slice of lemon in the microwave then wipe clean.

YOUR FREEZER

Whether you choose a chest or an upright freezer will depend on the quantity of food you wish to freeze, where the freezer will be placed and how often you use it. A chest freezer usually has a larger capacity and may freeze to a lower temperature. An upright freezer usually has easier access to the frozen foods. Whatever you decide, a freezer and the food in it are an investment in both money and time. Used well, they will save you both.

FILLING THE FREEZER

A freezer runs most economically when it is at least three-quarters full. There is less empty air to keep chilled and the frozen food helps to hold down the temperature. If you are planning a party, run down your stocks a little before you start to prepare and freeze the party foods. If you are a gardener or like to freeze fruits and vegetables in season, make sure you have plenty of space at the relevant times of year. If you like to take advantage of supermarket bargains, make sure you always have a little space for extra buys.

FREEZER TEMPERATURES
Storage and thawing times in this book are based on a freezer temperature of 17.7°C/0°F, which is attained by most chest or upright freezers. Freezer compartments of refrigerators are frequently at a higher temperature therefore are only suitable for short-term storage. You can check the temperature of your freezer by using an accurate freezer thermometer.

HOW TO FREEZE FOODS
If you are freezing cooked foods, leave them to cool then chill them in the refrigerator. Pack them carefully (see page 11) then place them in the freezer. You can freeze a single item without changing the controls or rearranging the food already in the freezer.

Foods which are frozen quickly form smaller ice crystals and retain their quality. If you are freezing in quantity, add only 1-1.5 kg/2-3 lb of frozen food per 30 cubic centimetres/1 cubic foot of freezer capacity. Before adding large quantities of food, clear enough space for the food. You can also check the food you already have in the freezer and move it to the most convenient position. Place unfrozen food in a single layer against the walls of the freezer or in the quick-freeze section. Allow 2.5 cm/1 in of air space between the packages so that the cold air can circulate. Allow 24 hours before restacking the food.

WHAT TO FREEZE
Freeze foods which you use regularly and not in too large quantities, so that you use them within the recommended storage times.

Freezing preserves the quality of foods if they are correctly packed and used within the recommended storage time. Microwave cooking brings out the flavour and texture. Neither will improve poor quality foods.

Buy vegetables in season when they are at their freshest and most flavoursome. Buy quality meat or poultry from a reputable butcher or supermarket.

If you buy meat in quantity, choose a butcher who specialises in meats for home freezers. Ask him to remove excess fat and large bones and have the meat cut and packaged for your family's taste and size. Ask the butcher to separate chops or steaks with freezer paper so that they can be separated for thawing. Make sure the packaging is good quality and the parcels are clearly labelled.

PACKING FOR THE FREEZER
In order for food to maintain its quality, it must be packed correctly in moisture-proof, airtight packaging which seals in the natural moisture in the food. If air can circulate round the food — either because it was trapped inside the packaging or has entered through inadequate wrapping or through a loose seal – it will draw moisture from the food and produce freezer burn, making

the food dry and tough.

In most cases, food is removed from the packaging before it is defrosted or reheated, so it is not essential to freeze in microwave containers; you can use any freezer-proof package. However, food thaws or reheats better when in a correctly sized container so it is a good idea to line the dish in which you intend to reheat the food with foil and freeze the food in the dish. Once frozen, you can remove the container.

1. Choose containers which are suitable for the freezer; materials suitable for refrigeration may not be appropriate.

2. Square or rectangular freezer boxes are easier to stack and store than round ones or irregularly-shaped items, and also have tight-fitting lids. Remember to leave enough head space for expansion when filling containers with foods in sauce. Plastic margarine or other cartons are not suitable on their own, but can be used to hold and shape airtight bags or can be overwrapped with foil, freezer paper or freezer bags. Waxed paper cartons can also be used in conjunction with freezer bags. Foil containers with card lids do not make an airtight seal so should be over-wrapped and sealed.

3. Freeze in quantities which reflect your own requirements: individual servings or double portions, for example, depending on the size of your family. If you generally freeze four servings, freeze a few individual servings for flexibility and convenience when entertaining or cooking for someone who needs to eat at a different time

from the rest of the family. If you have a large family, freeze two smaller packages. Smaller packages freeze faster and more efficiently than large ones. Small amounts also thaw and reheat more quickly and evenly. Separate steaks or chops with freezer paper.

4. Kitchen foil moulds tightly against food to create an airtight package but can tear in use. Pad sharp edges with crumpled foil before wrapping. Foil is excellent for lining casseroles.

5. Plastic freezer wrap makes a secure, airtight package but loosens in the freezer. Overwrap with foil or freezer paper.

6. Wax or plastic-coated freezer wrap should be used with the coated or shiny side against the food. Press out as much air as possible and seal the seams with freezer tape. You can write directly on to the paper.

7. Plastic freezer bags are convenient for all kinds of foods. Do use freezer quality bags as others are not moisture-proof in the freezer. Use bags large enough to enclose the food and allow sealing space at the top. Press the bag against the food or withdraw the air by sucking it out through a straw before sealing with a twist tie.

8. Store liquids in bags resting in a carton or square box to make them easier to store. Liquids expand during freezing so allow head space.

9. To pack main dishes, line a casserole with foil allowing a 3 cm/1½ in overlap. Spoon in the food

and freeze until firm. Remove from the dish and overwrap in a freezer bag or with freezer paper.

LABELLING

Always label food with the food, the date, and the quantity or number of servings before freezing it. The date can be the date on which the food was frozen, or the date by which the food should be used, but don't use a mixture or it will be confusing. Mystery packages are frustrating and waste time and freezer space. Use freezer labels or freezer tape and a waterproof marker.

Identify prepared foods with the recipe name and page so you can find thawing and heating directions quickly. Add any additional information such as ingredients which need to be added to complete the dish.

ORGANISING YOUR FREEZER

If your freezer is well organised, you will be able to find what you want, see what needs to be replaced and use the food regularly. It is a waste of space to have items sitting in the freezer which are not regularly eaten.

1. Allocate sections of your freezer to types of food so that you know where to find things.

2. Use baskets, shelves or dividers, depending on your type of freezer, to separate different foods.

3. Use an open box, basket or bag to store small or irregularly-shaped items more easily.

4. Rearrange foods regularly, checking dates and moving older items to the top or front where you can use them first.

5. Keep a freezer notebook to record foods frozen, the date and quantity. Cross them off when you use them. Before buying new stocks, check through your notebook to see what you already have.

POWER FAILURES

If the freezer stops working, leave the door closed to keep the chilled air inside; the food will stay frozen for some time. How long will depend on the weather, the location and size of the freezer and how full it is. In a full-packed freezer at 17.7°C/0°F, food will not start to defrost for 12 hours. Your house contents insurance or insurance taken out with your freezer may cover food spoiled by this occurrence.

Food should not be refrozen once thawed or partially thawed.

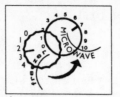

chapter 3

STORAGE TIMES FOR FROZEN FOODS

Uncooked Foods	Maximum Storage Time
Fish and Shellfish	
Whole oily fish	*2 months*
Whole white fish	*3 months*
Shellfish	*1 month*
Meat, Poultry and Game	
Bacon joints	*5 weeks*
rashers	*3 months*
Beef joints	*8 months*
mince / sausages	*3 months*
steaks	*6 months*

Uncooked Foods	Maximum Storage Time
Lamb joints	*8 months*
chops / cutlets	*6 months*
Pork joints	*6 months*
chops	*3 months*
sausages	*2 months*
Veal joints	*6 months*
mince / cubes	*3 months*
Chicken	*12 months*
Duck	*6 months*
Goose	*4 months*
Rabbit / Game	*6 months*
Turkey	*6 months*
Offal	*3 months*
Vegetables	
Most vegetables	*12 months*
Artichokes	*3 months*
Avocado Pear	*2 months*
Beetroot	*6 months*
Cauliflower	*6 months*
Herbs	*6 months*
Leeks	*6 months*
Mushrooms	*1 month*
Fruit	
Juice	*6 months*
Fruit with sugar	*9 months*
Fruit without sugar	*3 months*
Purées	*6 months*

Uncooked Foods	Maximum Storage Time
Dairy Produce	
Butter, unsalted	*12 months*
salted	*6 months*
Cheese	*4 months*
Cream	*4 months*
Eggs	*6 months*
Ice cream	*1 month*
Margarine	*5 months*
Baked Goods	
Biscuits	*6 months*
Bread	*6 months*
Cakes	*3 months*
Flans	
unfilled / unbaked	*3 months*
Pastry	
unbaked	*3 months*
baked	*6 months*
Puddings	*3 months*
Scones	*6 months*

Cooked Foods	Maximum Storage Time
Casseroles	*2-4 months*
Bacon joints	*1 month*
Fish dishes	*1-2 months*
Pâtés	*1 month*
Pies	*2 months*
Soups	*2 months*

c h a p t e r   4

THAWING FOODS

Starting temperatures are important in both microwave cooking and thawing. You already know that refrigerated food takes longer to cook than food at room temperature, and the same is true of frozen food. Food frozen to a lower temperature will take longer to thaw. Times in this book are based on a freezer temperature of 17.7°C/0°F. If your freezer has a higher temperature thawing times may be shorter. If the freezer temperature is lower, thawing times may be longer, although the food will also last longer in the freezer.

Thaw foods in the microwave using the Low or Defrost setting. On these settings, the power is switched on and off so that the smaller ice crystals which are defrosted by the microwaves transmit their heat to the larger crystals during resting and ensure even thawing. If you do not have these settings, microwave on High for about 30 seconds then switch off for about 1½ minutes and continue until the food is thawed.

1. Foods should be thawed completely before cooking to ensure best results.

2. Cover food except baking goods during thawing but open cartons or pierce plastic coverings.

3. Separate foods, such as chops, as they thaw.

4. Arrange foods with the denser areas to the outside and without overlapping.

5. Remove large lumps of ice before thawing.

6. Use a suitable microwave container in which the food fits neatly. Foods which are thawed in their cold freezer container may take longer to defrost.

7. Turn, rearrange or stir foods during thawing to break them up.

8. Always remove foods from metal containers or remove freezer wrap before thawing.

9. Place foods such as cakes on kitchen paper.

10. Allow a standing time after thawing.

REHEATING COOKED DISHES

When preparing cooked dishes, freeze them in a suitable container or line the container with foil, freeze the dish then remove the container so that you can use it again. You can then simply remove the foil and return the food to the container ready for the microwave. Always thaw foods before you reheat them to ensure best results. Reheating times will vary depending on the starting temperature of the food (see Thawing Foods).

1. Always underestimate reheating times, especially for vegetables and small portions of food. Many foods reheat very quickly and will spoil if overcooked.

2. Wrap foods in microwave film or cover them before reheating.

3. Stand baked goods on kitchen paper to absorb moisture.

4. Slice meats to reheat more quickly.

5. Arrange foods as you would for cooking or thawing with the densest parts of the food on the edges.

6. Use suitable microwave containers.

7. Stir or rearrange foods during reheating.

8. Pies which are warm outside may be very hot inside. Take care when serving and eating.

9. Reheating foods in sauce ensures even heating and prevents them from drying out.

10. Leave foods to stand for a few moments before serving.

chapter 6

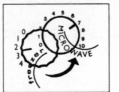

YOUR FREEZER-MICROWAVE PARTNERSHIP

A little thought goes a long way when you are planning to get the best out of your freezer and your microwave oven as a partnership. Here are a few tips to set you thinking.

1. Cook extra quantities so that you can freeze and reheat meals for convenience.

2. Pack freezer foods in microwave containers so they can go straight into the oven, or line microwave containers with foil and freeze the meal, so that it can be unwrapped and placed back into the original dish.

3. Freeze in quantities appropriate to your needs.

4. Prepare sauces in the microwave which can be frozen then reheated all in the same container.

5. Write reheating or finishing instructions on your freezer labels.

6. The recipes are written so that you have all the cooking instructions in the main method. If you are intending to freeze the dish, check the freezing instructions as some dishes are best frozen without particular ingredients. You can then complete the cooking when the dish is required.

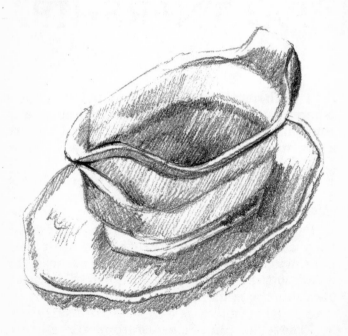

chapter 7

MEAT

There are many ways to take advantage of your freezer and microwave for main courses, buying meat for freezing or freezing ready-made dishes for reheating whenever you need them.

PACKAGING FOR THE FREEZER
Supermarket-wrapped meat is not sufficiently airtight for the freezer so rewrap in foil, freezer wrap or freezer bags. Divide large quantities into meal-sized amounts. Some butchers will freezer-wrap meat for you on request.

THAWING
Careful thawing is essential otherwise meat loses its moisture. With a microwave, you can thaw the meat as you need it and avoid moisture loss, which detracts from the quality of the meat. Remove the packing before you start to thaw. The packing holds juices against the surface of the meat and can cause the surface to start to cook before the centre is defrosted. Stand roasts, steaks and chops on a rack to keep them out of

their juices. If the wrap sticks to the meat, put the wrapped package in the microwave, start defrosting, and remove the wrapping as soon as possible. Leave the meat to stand only until the centre can be pierced with a skewer. The meat should still feel cold.

To thaw large joints remove the packing and place the meat on a rack. Thaw for a quarter of the total time indicated in the chart on page 27. Feel the joint for warm areas and shield these with pieces of foil. Turn the joint over and thaw for the second quarter of the total time or until the surface of the meat yields to pressure. Leave to stand for 10 minutes.

Turn the joint over again and continue to thaw for another quarter of the total time. Feel again for warm areas and shield these with foil. Turn the joint and thaw for the remaining time. Leave to stand for 20-30 minutes or until a skewer can be inserted into the centre.

Separate steaks and chops after unwrapping and thaw on a rack for half the total time indicated in the chart on page 27. Turn over and defrost for the remaining time. Leave to stand for 5 minutes until the meat is pliable.

Remove the packing from minced meat and place the meat in a dish. Thaw for one-third of the total time indicated in the chart. Turn the meat over and scrape off any soft pieces. Thaw for the second one-third of the total time. Scrape off and remove soft pieces and break up the remaining meat with a fork. Thaw for the remaining time. Leave to stand for 5-10 minutes until softened but still cold.

MEAT THAWING TIMES

Type	Thawing Time on Medium
Beef joints	*5 $\frac{1}{2}$-6 $\frac{1}{2}$ mins per 450 g / 1 lb*
steaks	*3-4 mins per 450 g / 1 lb*
mince	*3-5 mins per 450 g / 1 lb*
Pork joints	*6-9 mins per 450 g / 1 lb*
chops	*3 $\frac{1}{2}$-6 mins per 450 g / 1 lb*
mince	*3-5 mins per 450 g / 1 lb*
Lamb joints	*5-8 mins per 450 g / 1 lb*
chops	*4-6 $\frac{1}{2}$ mins per 450 g / 1 lb*
Sausages / sausagemeat	*3-5 mins per 450 g / 1 lb*

BEEF AND BEAN STEW

Serves 6

Ingredients	Metric	Imperial	American
Minced (ground) beef	*225 g*	*8 oz*	*1/2 lb*
Onion, sliced	*1*	*1*	*1*
Green pepper, chopped	*1*	*1*	*1*
Dried thyme	*2.5 ml*	*1/2 tsp*	*1/2 tsp*
Canned tomatoes, chopped	*500 g*	*18 oz*	*18 oz*
Boiled potatoes, sliced	*450 g*	*1 lb*	*1 lb*
Canned kidney beans, rinsed and drained	*450 g*	*1 lb*	*1lb*
Beef stock	*450 ml*	*3/4 pt*	*2 cups*
Chilli powder	*10 ml*	*2 tsp*	*2 tsp*
Salt			
Cornflour (cornstarch)	*10 ml*	*2 tsp*	*2 tsp*
Water	*15 ml*	*1 tbsp*	*1 tbsp*

Put the beef, onion, pepper and thyme in a large casserole, cover and microwave on High for 7 minutes until the onion is tender, stirring 2 or 3 times during cooking. Add all the remaining ingredients except the cornflour and water and mix well. Cover and microwave on High for 15-20 minutes until hot, stirring 2 or 3 times during cooking. If the sauce has not thickened to your taste, blend the cornflour and the water to a paste, stir into the casserole and microwave on High for a further 2 minutes until thick.

To Freeze: Freeze the finished dish for up to 4 months.

To Serve: Transfer to a casserole dish and thaw on Defrost or Low for 15-20 minutes, stand for 8-10 minutes then reheat on High for about 10 minutes until hot, stirring occasionally during cooking.

BEEF IN WINE

Serves 4 – 6

Ingredients	Metric	Imperial	American
Onion, cut into rings	*1*	*1*	*1*
Celery stick, sliced	*1*	*1*	*1*
Butter or margarine	*15 ml*	*1 tbsp*	*1 tbsp*
Steak, cut into strips	*675 g*	*1 ¹/₂ lb*	*1 ¹/₂ lb*
Red wine	*175 ml*	*6 fl oz*	*³/₄ cup*
Beef stock cube	*¹/₂*	*¹/₂*	*¹/₂*
Dried parsley	*1 tsp*	*1 tsp*	*1 tsp*
Salt and pepper			
To Serve			
Plain flour	*15 ml*	*1 tbsp*	*1 tbsp*
Water	*45 ml*	*3 tbsp*	*3 tbsp*

Put the onion, celery and butter or margarine in a casserole dish, cover and microwave on High for 4 minutes.
Stir in the remaining ingredients, except the flour and
water. Cover and microwave on Medium-High for 18-25
minutes until the meat is tender, stirring 2 or 3 times
during cooking. Remove the meat and vegetables with a
slotted spoon. Blend the flour and water and stir into
the remaining liquid, adding a little more water if necessary. Microwave on High for 3 ¹/₂-5 ¹/₂ minutes until
thickened, stirring once or twice. Return the meat and
vegetables to the sauce. Serve with rice or noodles.

To Freeze: Prepare the ingredients, cook the onion and
celery and mix in the remaining ingredients except the
flour and water. Freeze before cooking for up to 4
months.

To Serve: Transfer to a casserole dish and thaw on
Defrost or Low for 10-15 minutes, stand for 8-10
minutes then proceed with the recipe.

BEEF AND VEGETABLES

Serves 4 – 6

Ingredients	Metric	Imperial	American
Frozen topside of beef	*1-1.5 kg*	*2 ¹/₂-3 lb*	*2 ¹/₂-3 lb*
Dry sherry	*60 ml*	*4 tbsp*	*4 tbsp*
Chilli sauce	*45 ml*	*3 tbsp*	*3 tbsp*
Pinch of mustard powder			
Pinch of dried rosemary			
Dried mixed herbs	*2.5 ml*	*¹/₂ tsp*	*¹/₂ tsp*
Carrot, thinly sliced	*1*	*1*	*1*
Onion, thinly sliced	*1*	*1*	*1*
Small turnip, thinly sliced	*1*	*1*	*1*
Small parsnip, sliced	*1*	*1*	*1*
Plain flour	*30 ml*	*2 tbsp*	*2 tbsp*
Cold water	*75 ml*	*5 tbsp*	*5 tbsp*

Unwrap the roast and put it in a baking dish. Cover with plastic wrap. Microwave on Medium for 35 minutes. Turn over. Mix together the sherry, chilli sauce, mustard, rosemary and herbs. Pour the mixture over the roast. Arrange the carrot, onion, turnip and parsnip around the meat. Cover with plastic wrap.

Microwave on Medium for 1-1 ¹/₄ hours until the meat is tender in the centre, turning the meat once or twice during cooking. Cover and leave to stand for 5 minutes. Put the roast on a serving dish, cover with foil and leave to one side.

Mix together the flour and water and stir into the vegetables in the dish. Microwave on High for 3 ¹/₂ -6 minutes until thickened, stirring 2 or 3 times during cooking. Serve with mashed or boiled potatoes.

To Freeze: Freeze before thickening the sauce for up to 4 months.

To Serve: Thaw on Defrost or Low for 10 minutes, stand for 10 minutes then reheat on High for 10-15 minutes. Remove the meat and thicken the sauce as above.

BEEF STROGANOFF

Serves 4 – 6

Ingredients	Metric	Imperial	American
Button mushrooms, halved	225 g	8 oz	1/2 lb
Onion, chopped	1	1	1
Butter or margarine	15 ml	1 tbsp	1 tbsp
Rump steak, cut into thin strips	675 g	1 1/2 lb	1 1/2 lb
White wine	150 ml	1/4 pt	2/3 cup
Canned tomatoes, sieved	120 ml	4 fl oz	2/3 cup
Beef stock cube	1	1	1
Salt and pepper			
To Serve			
Plain flour	45 ml	3 tbsp	3 tbsp
Water	75 ml	5 tbsp	5 tbsp
Soured cream	120 ml	4 fl oz	1/2 cup
Tomato ketchup (catsup)	15 ml	1 tbsp	1 tbsp

Put the mushrooms, onion and butter or margarine into a casserole. Cover and microwave on High for 4-8 minutes until the onion is tender. Stir in the steak, wine, tomato juice, stock cube, salt and pepper. Cover and microwave on High for 5 minutes. Reduce the power to Medium and microwave for 22-30 minutes until the beef is tender, stirring 2 or 3 times.

Using a slotted spoon transfer the beef to a bowl and cover loosely with foil. Blend the flour and water and stir into the meat juices in the casserole. Microwave on High for 5-8 minutes until thickened, stirring 2 or 3 times. Stir the beef into the sauce. Stir in the soured cream and ketchup. Serve with rice or noodles.

To Freeze: Spoon into a rigid container before thickening the sauce and freeze for up to 4 months.

To Serve: Transfer to a casserole dish, cover and microwave on Medium for 25-35 minutes until thoroughly heated, stirring 2 or 3 times. Thicken the sauce as above and season with soured cream and ketchup.

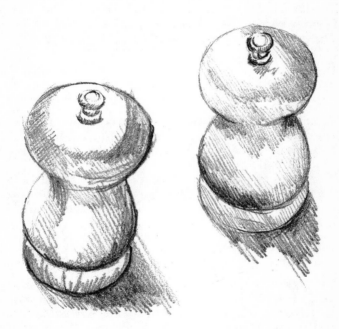

CHILLI CON CARNE

Serves 4

Ingredients	Metric	Imperial	American
Minced (ground) beef	*450 g*	*1 lb*	*1 lb*
Onions, chopped	*2*	*2*	*2*
Canned tomatoes	*400 g*	*15 oz*	*15 oz*
Canned red kidney			
beans, drained	*400 g*	*15 oz*	*15 oz*
Canned passata	*300 g*	*11 oz*	*11 oz*
Chilli powder	*15 ml*	*1 tbsp*	*1 tbsp*
Ground cumin	*5 ml*	*1 tsp*	*1 tsp*
Paprika	*5 ml*	*1 tsp*	*1 tsp*
Salt and pepper			

Crumble the minced beef into a large casserole dish with the onions, cover and microwave on High for 6-8 minutes until the meat is no longer pink, stirring 2 or 3 times. Drain.

Stir in the remaining ingredients. Cover and microwave on High for 10 minutes. Stir. Reduce the power to Medium, uncover and microwave for 25-35 minutes until slightly thickened.

To Freeze: Freeze in a rigid container for up to 4 months.

To Serve: Transfer to a casserole dish, cover and thaw on Defrost or Low for 8-10 minutes, stand for 8-10 minutes then reheat on Medium for 10-15 minutes until heated, breaking apart with a fork as soon as possible and stirring once or twice.

SPICY MEATBALLS

Serves 4 – 6

Ingredients	Metric	Imperial	American
Meatballs			
Onion, chopped	*1*	*1*	*1*
Garlic cloves, crushed	*2*	*2*	*2*
Olive oil	*15 ml*	*1 tbsp*	*1 tbsp*
Minced (ground) beef	*450 g*	*1 lb*	*1 lb*
Dry breadcrumbs	*50 g*	*2 oz*	*1/2 cup*
Mustard powder	*5 ml*	*1 tsp*	*1 tsp*
Salt and pepper			
Egg, beaten	*1*	*1*	*1*
For The Sauce			
Tomato sauce	*300 ml*	*1/2 pt*	*1 1/4 cups*
(see page 148)			
Chopped fresh parsley	*15 ml*	*1 tbsp*	*1 tbsp*
Sugar	*2.5 ml*	*1/2 tsp*	*1/2 tsp*

Put the onion, garlic and olive oil into a medium-sized
bowl and microwave on High for 3 minutes until the
onion is tender. Stir in the remaining meatball ingredients. Shape into small balls and arrange on a
baking dish. Cover and microwave on High for 4-5 1/2
minutes until set but still slightly pink, rearranging and
turning over after half the time. Drain.

Combine the sauce ingredients in a small bowl.
Microwave on High for 1-2 1/2 minutes until heated.

To Freeze: Arrange the meatballs so that they do not
touch each other on a tray lined with waxed paper.
Freeze until firm then pack and freeze for up to 1
month. Freeze the sauce separately.

To Serve: Thaw the meatballs in 2 or 3 batches, cover
and microwave on Medium-High for 8-14 minutes until
meatballs are defrosted. Thaw the sauce on Medium for
about 6-8 minutes, stirring occasionally, until heated.

STUFFED PEPPERS

Serves 4

Ingredients	Metric	Imperial	American
Medium red or green			
peppers	*4*	*4*	*4*
Onion, sliced	*1*	*1*	*1*
Garlic cloves, sliced	*2*	*2*	*2*
Mushrooms, sliced	*100 g*	*4 oz*	*¼ lb*
Vegetable oil	*30 ml*	*2 tbsp*	*2 tbsp*
Cooked long-grain rice	*60 ml*	*4 tbsp*	*4 tbsp*
Sunflower seeds	*30 ml*	*2 tbsp*	*2 tbsp*
Salt	*5 ml*	*1 tsp*	*1 tsp*
Pepper			
Ground cumin	*2.5 ml*	*½ tsp*	*½ tsp*
Vegetable stock	*60 ml*	*4 tbsp*	*4 tbsp*

Halve the peppers. Wash and remove seeds and internal fibres and arrange in a dish.

Place the onion, garlic and mushrooms in a bowl, sprinkle with oil, cover and microwave on High for 3 minutes. Stir in the rice, sunflower seeds and seasonings. Stuff the peppers with this mixture. Carefully put the two halves together. Sprinkle the vegetable stock over the peppers and microwave on High for 10 minutes.

To Freeze: Pack in a rigid container and freeze for up to 1 month.

To Serve: Thaw on Defrost or Low for 5-8 minutes, stand for 8 minutes then reheat on High for 6-10 minutes until heated through, rearranging once or twice.

BAKED PORK LOAF

Serves 4 – 6

Ingredients	Metric	Imperial	American
Garlic clove, crushed	1	1	1
Courgette, grated	1	1	1
Button mushrooms, sliced	100 g	4 oz	1/4 lb
Grated Parmesan cheese	30 ml	2 tbsp	2 tbsp
Oregano	5 ml	1 tsp	1 tsp
Salt and pepper			
Minced (ground) pork	450 g	1 lb	1 lb
Sausagemeat	225 g	8 oz	1/2 lb
Butter or margarine	30 ml	2 tbsp	2 tbsp
Dry breadcrumbs	45 ml	3 tbsp	3 tbsp
Paprika	2.5 ml	1/2 tsp	1/2 tsp

Put the garlic, courgette and mushrooms into a small bowl. Microwave on High for 2 minutes. Drain. Stir in cheese, oregano, salt and pepper. Set aside.

In a medium bowl, mix together the pork and sausagemeat. Spoon alternate layers of the meat mixture and the courgette mixture into a microwave loaf tin.

Put the butter in a small bowl. Microwave on High for 30-45 seconds until butter melts. Mix in the breadcrumbs and paprika. Sprinkle over the loaf.

To Freeze: Assemble the loaf and freeze before cooking for 2 months.

To Serve: Thaw on Defrost or Low for 10-12 minutes, stand for 10-12 minutes then reheat on Medium for 30-40 minutes until cooked through turning several times during cooking.

CHINESE-STYLE SPARE RIBS

Serves 4

Ingredients	Metric	Imperial	American
Pork spare ribs	*1.5 kg*	*3 lb*	*3 lb*
Hot water	*150 ml*	*¼ pt*	*¾ cup*
Onion, sliced into			
rings	*1*	*1*	*1*
Garlic clove, crushed	*1*	*1*	*1*
Dried thyme	*2.5 ml*	*½ tsp*	*½ tsp*
For The Sauce			
Soy sauce	*110 ml*	*4 fl oz*	*½ cup*
Brown sugar	*50 g*	*2 oz*	*¼ cup*
Dry sherry	*30 ml*	*2 tbsp*	*2 tbsp*
Chopped crystallised			
ginger	*30 ml*	*2 tbsp*	*2 tbsp*
Five-spice powder	*5 ml*	*1 tsp*	*1 tsp*
Salt	*5 ml*	*1 tsp*	*1 tsp*

Chop the spare ribs into 2 or 3 sections and put into a large casserole dish with the water, onion, garlic and thyme. Cover and microwave on High for 5 minutes. Reduce the power to Medium and microwave for 40-60 minutes until the ribs are tender, rearranging 2 or 3 times during cooking. Cover and leave to stand for 5-10 minutes.

In a medium bowl, mix together all the sauce ingredients. Microwave on High for 2-4 minutes until the sugar has dissolved, stirring once or twice.

Put the ribs under a medium-hot grill and brush with the sauce. Grill for 15-30 minutes until the sauce is set, brushing with sauce and turning the ribs over 2 or 3 times.

To Freeze: Open freeze on a tray then pack and freeze for up to 2 months.

To Serve: Unwrap and place on a baking sheet. Cover with waxed paper and microwave on Medium for 8-13 minutes until heated, rearranging once or twice.

PORK IN CIDER

Serves 4

Ingredients	Metric	Imperial	American
Lean pork, cubed	450 g	1 lb	1 lb
Dry cider	300 ml	1/2 pt	1 1/4 cups
Plain flour	15 ml	1 tbsp	1 tbsp
Cayenne pepper	5 ml	1 tsp	1 tsp
Salt and pepper			
Onion, sliced	1	1	1
Carrots, sliced	2	2	2
Bay leaf	1	1	1
Mushrooms, sliced	100 g	4 oz	1/4 lb
Chopped fresh parsley	15 ml	1 tbsp	1 tbsp

Marinate the pork in the cider for several hours. Drain, reserving the cider. Season the flour with cayenne, salt and pepper then toss the meat in the flour. Shake off any excess. Place the onion and carrots in a casserole dish and add the meat and bay leaf. Pour over the cider, cover and microwave on High for 10 minutes, stirring twice during cooking. Microwave on Medium for 25-30 minutes until the meat is tender. Stir in the mushrooms and leave to stand for 10 minutes. Check for seasoning and serve garnished with parsley.

To Freeze: Remove the bay leaf and freeze in a rigid container for up to 3 months.

To Serve: Transfer to a casserole dish, cover and thaw on Defrost or Low for 8-10 minutes, breaking apart with a fork as soon as possible. Stand for 5 minutes and microwave on Medium - High for 8-10 minutes.

ORIENTAL PORK

Serves 4

Ingredients	Metric	Imperial	American
Oil	*15 ml*	*1 tbsp*	*1 tbsp*
Onion, chopped	*1*	*1*	*1*
Carrot, cut into strips	*1*	*1*	*1*
Green pepper, cut into strips	*1*	*1*	*1*
Celery stick, sliced	*1*	*1*	*1*
Lean pork, cubed	*450 g*	*1 lb*	*1 lb*
Canned tomatoes, sieved	*400 g*	*14 oz*	*14 oz*
Tomato purée (paste)	*15 ml*	*1 tbsp*	*1 tbsp*
Vinegar	*30 ml*	*2 tbsp*	*2 tbsp*
Light soft brown sugar	*15 ml*	*1 tbsp*	*1 tbsp*
Chicken stock	*300 ml*	*1/2 pt*	*1 1/4 cups*
Plum jam	*15 ml*	*1 tbsp*	*1 tbsp*
Salt and pepper			
Cornflour (cornstarch)	*10 ml*	*2 tsp*	*2 tsp*

Put the oil into a casserole with the onion, carrot, pepper, and celery and microwave on High for 5 minutes, stirring twice. Add the pork and microwave on High for 2 minutes. Add the tomatoes, tomato purée, vinegar, sugar, stock, jam and seasoning. Cover and microwave for 20-25 minutes, stirring twice. Mix the cornflour with a little water and stir into the casserole. Microwave on High for 2 minutes, stirring twice. Leave to stand for 10 minutes.

To Freeze: Freeze in a rigid container for up to 2 months.

To Serve: Thaw on Defrost or Low for 8-10 minutes, stand for 5 minutes then reheat on High for 8-10 minutes.

QUICK PORK CASSEROLE

Serves 4

Ingredients	Metric	Imperial	American
Potato, cubed	*1*	*1*	*1*
Carrot, thinly sliced	*1*	*1*	*1*
Celery stick, sliced	*1*	*1*	*1*
Butter or margarine	*30 ml*	*2 tbsp*	*2 tbsp*
Chopped fresh parsley	*30 ml*	*2 tbsp*	*2 tbsp*
Canned tomatoes, chopped	*400 g*	*15 oz*	*15 oz*
Cooked pork, cubed	*450 g*	*1 lb*	*1 lb*
Dried sage	*2.5 ml*	*1/2 tsp*	*1/2 tsp*
Salt and pepper			
To Serve			
Plain flour	*30 ml*	*2 tbsp*	*2 tbsp*
White wine	*60 ml*	*4 tbsp*	*4 tbsp*

Put the potato, carrot, celery and butter or margarine into a casserole dish, cover and microwave on High for 3-5 minutes until the vegetables are still crisp, stirring once. Add the parsley, tomatoes, pork, sage, salt and pepper.

Drain off a little of the cooking juices and mix them with the flour and wine in a small bowl. Microwave on High for 2-4 minutes until thickened, stirring once or twice. Stir into the casserole, cover and microwave on Medium-High for 10-14 minutes until hot, stirring once or twice. Serve with rice.

To Freeze: Freeze before thickening the sauce for up to 2 months.

To Serve: Transfer to a casserole dish, cover and thaw on Defrost or Low for 10-14 minutes, breaking apart with a fork as soon as possible. Stand for 8 minutes. Prepare the thickening sauce and proceed with the recipe.

SAUSAGEMEAT BAKE

Serves 6 – 8

Ingredients	Metric	Imperial	American
Tomato, skinned and finely chopped	*1*	*1*	*1*
Onion, finely chopped	*1*	*1*	*1*
Garlic clove, crushed	*1*	*1*	*1*
Celery stick, finely chopped	*1*	*1*	*1*
Sausagemeat	*450 g*	*1 lb*	*1 lb*
Minced (ground) beef	*225 g*	*8 oz*	*1/2 lb*
Eggs, lightly beaten	*2*	*2*	*2*
Dry breadcrumbs	*75 g*	*3 oz*	*3/4 cup*
Dried sage	*1/2 tsp*	*1/2 tsp*	*1/2 tsp*
Cooked ham, minced	*100 g*	*4 oz*	*1/4 lb*

Put the tomato, onion, garlic and celery into a casserole, cover and microwave on High for 4-6 minutes until soft, stirring once. Mix in the remaining ingredients except the ham. Spread half the mixture in a foil-lined loaf tin. Spread the ham over the top to within 1 cm/¹⁄₂ in of the edge. Spread with remaining sausage mixture, and press down. Microwave on Medium-High for 10 minutes. Shield the top edges with 2.5 cm/1 in wide strips of foil and microwave on Medium-High for 25-30 minutes until cooked through. Cover and leave to stand for 10 minutes.

To Freeze: Assemble in the loaf tin and freeze, before cooking, for up to 2 months.

To Serve: Thaw on Defrost or Low for 6-8 minutes, leave to stand for 6-8 minutes then continue with the recipe.

FRUITY PORK

Serves 4 – 6

Ingredients	Metric	Imperial	American
Water	120 ml	4 fl oz	1/2 cup
White wine vinegar	60 ml	4 tbsp	4 tbsp
Golden syrup	30 ml	2 tbsp	2 tbsp
Soy sauce	15 ml	1 tbsp	1 tbsp
Pepper			
Boneless pork, cut into thin strips	450 g	1 lb	1 lb
Apple, chopped	1	1	1
Mixed nuts, chopped	25 g	1 oz	1/4 cup
Sultanas (golden raisins)	30 ml	2 tbsp	2 tbsp
To Serve			
Canned mandarin oranges	300 g	11 oz	11 oz
Cornflour (cornstarch)	15 ml	1 tbsp	1 tbsp

Mix the water, wine vinegar, syrup, soy sauce and pepper in a casserole dish and Microwave on High for 1-2 minutes until blended, stirring once. Stir in the pork, cover and leave to stand for 1 hour.

Drain, reserving 30 ml/2 tbsp of the marinade. Microwave, uncovered, on Medium-High for 4-6 minutes until the meat is no longer pink, stirring once. Add the reserved marinade, the apple, nuts and sultanas, cover and microwave on Medium-High for 10-12 minutes. Drain off the liquid into a bowl. Drain the mandarin oranges, reserving 60 ml/4 tbsp of juice. Stir the oranges into the casserole, cover and leave to stand. Blend the cornflour with the orange juice and stir into the reserved liquid. Microwave on High for 2-3 minutes until thick, stirring 2 or 3 times. Stir into the casserole. Serve with rice.

To Freeze: Freeze after adding the marinade and fruit, but before cooking in a rigid container for up to 2 months.

To Serve: Transfer to a casserole dish and thaw on Defrost or Low for 12-15 minutes, leave to stand for 8-10 minutes then continue with the recipe.

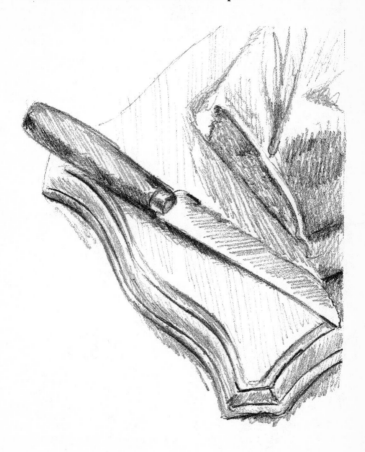

APPLE GAMMON

Serves 4

Ingredients	Metric	Imperial	American
Gammon steaks,	4 x	4 x	4 x
rinded	175 g	6 oz	6 oz
Onion, chopped	1	1	1
Dry cider	300 ml	$^1/_2$ pt	1 $^1/_4$ cups
Eating apple, peeled,			
cored and sliced	1	1	1
Sage leaves, chopped	2	2	2
Salt and pepper			

Put the steaks in a casserole dish in a single layer and microwave on High for 6-8 minutes, turning once. Add the onion and microwave on High for 3-4 minutes. Add the cider, apple and sage, salt and pepper and microwave on High for 7-8 minutes, stirring twice. Leave to stand for 5 minutes before serving.

To Freeze: Freeze for up to 2 months.

To Serve: Thaw on Defrost or Low for 8-10 minutes, leave to stand for 10 minutes, then reheat on High for 8-10 minutes.

LAMB CHOPS IN FRUIT SAUCE

Serves 4

Ingredients	Metric	Imperial	American
Lamb chops	8	8	8
Butter or margarine	15 ml	1 tbsp	1 tbsp
Onion, chopped	1	1	1
Clove garlic, crushed	1	1	1
Cornflour (cornstarch)	5 ml	1 tsp	1 tsp
Honey	15 ml	1 tbsp	1 tbsp
Mustard	5 ml	1 tsp	1 tsp
Dessert apple, peeled, cored and chopped	1	1	1
Raisins	50 g	2 oz	1/3 cup
Dry cider	150 ml	1/4 pt	2/3 cup
Salt and pepper			

Arrange the chops in a large shallow container, dot with butter or margarine, cover and cook on High for 8-10 minutes, turning over half way. Transfer to a serving plate, cover with foil and leave to stand for 10 minutes.

Stir the onion and garlic into the lamb juices, cover and cook on High for 3-4 minutes. Stir in the remaining ingredients, cover and cook on High for 5 minutes. Pour over the chops and serve with steamed vegetables.

To Freeze: Freeze the sauce with the chops for up to 2 months.

To Serve: Thaw on Defrost or Low for 10 minutes, stand for 10 minutes, then reheat on High for 8-10 minutes.

GINGERED LAMB CHOPS

Serves 4

Ingredients	Metric	Imperial	American
Lamb chump chops	4	4	4
Butter or margarine	50 g	2 oz	1/4 cup
Lemon juice	15 ml	1 tbsp	1 tbsp
Grated lemon rind	10 ml	2 tsp	2 tsp
Ground ginger	5 ml	1 tsp	1 tsp
Garlic clove, crushed	1/2	1/2	1/2
Salt and pepper			

Put the chops into a shallow dish. Put the butter into a bowl and microwave on High for 1 minute. Add the lemon juice and rind, ginger, garlic and seasoning and mix well. Spread on both sides of the chops. Microwave on High for 10-12 minutes, turning the chops 3 times during cooking. Serve with vegetables or a salad.

To Freeze: Freeze with waxed paper between the chops for up to 2 months.

To Serve: Separate the chops and thaw on Defrost or Low for 5 minutes, leave to stand for 5 minutes then reheat on High for 5-6 minutes.

LAMB STEW

Serves 4 – 6

Ingredients	Metric	Imperial	American
Cornflour	30 ml	2 tbsp	2 tbsp
Salt and pepper			
Boneless lamb, cubed	450 g	1 lb	1 lb
Potatoes, peeled and cubed	2	2	2
Carrot, diced	1	1	1
Onion, chopped	1	1	1
Beef stock, hot	175 ml	6 fl oz	3/4 cup
Chopped fresh parsley	15 ml	1 tbsp	1 tbsp
Bay leaf, crumbled	1	1	1
Apple, peeled, cored and diced	1	1	1
Frozen peas	175 g	6 oz	6 oz

Put the cornflour, salt and pepper into large casserole. Add the lamb and toss to coat. Stir in the remaining ingredients except the apples and peas, cover and microwave on High for 10 minutes. Stir. Reduce the power to Medium and microwave, covered, for 30 minutes, stirring 2 or 3 times. Add the apples and peas, cover and microwave on Medium for 15-20 minutes until the meat and vegetables are tender, stirring 2 or 3 times.

To Freeze: Freeze in a rigid container for up to 4 months.

To Serve: Transfer to a casserole dish, cover and microwave on Medium for 20-25 minutes until heated, breaking apart as soon as possible and stirring 3 or 4 times during cooking.

HERBED LIVER

Serves 4

Ingredients	Metric	Imperial	American
Butter or margarine	*30 ml*	*2 tbsp*	*2 tbsp*
Oil	*15 ml*	*1 tbsp*	*1 tbsp*
Onion, chopped	*1*	*1*	*1*
Streaky bacon			
* rashers, chopped*	*2*	*2*	*2*
Lambs' liver, sliced	*350 g*	*12 oz*	*12 oz*
Canned tomatoes,			
* chopped or sieved*	*400 g*	*14 oz*	*14 oz*
Mixed herbs	*5 ml*	*1 tsp*	*1 tsp*
Salt and pepper			

Put the butter or margarine and oil in a casserole and microwave on High for 2 minutes. Add the onion and bacon and continue cooking for 3 minutes, stirring once. Add the liver and cook for 1 minute. Add the tomatoes, herbs and seasoning. Microwave on High for 7 minutes, stirring twice. Leave to stand for 5 minutes before serving.

To Freeze: Freeze in a rigid container for up to 2 months.

To Serve: Thaw on Defrost or Low for 8-10 minutes, stand for 8-10 minutes then reheat on High for 8 minutes.

VEGETABLES

The speedy microwave cooking of vegetables preserves their flavour, colour and texture. You can also use the microwave to blanch fresh vegetables for freezing.

PACKING FOR THE FREEZER

Blanching inactivates the enzymes which cause vegetables to lose vitamins, flavour and colour. Vegetables blanched at the peak of freshness and flavour retain quality and vitamin content. If you are a gardener, harvest vegetables as they reach their peak rather than trying to preserve the whole crop at one time.

When you wish to blanch several batches, prepare the second while the first is in the oven. Don't try to increase the quantities done at one time. Cook green vegetables only until the colour brightens. Other vegetables should remain very crisp.

Freezing water in plastic ice cream tubs is a convenient way of making ice for cooling the vegetables quickly. Freeze water several days before you plan to use it. Have iced water ready in the sink or a large container before micro-waving the vegetables.

Clean the vegetables thoroughly and cut into small slices, cubes or florets so the vegetables blanch and freeze evenly. Put the vegetables into a casserole with a little water, cover and microwave as directed in the chart until the vegetables are soft but crisp and the colour brightens. Drain the vegetables and plunge immediately into iced water to stop the cooking process. Cool completely and drain thoroughly.

Pack small amounts into freezer bags, boxes or small containers, leaving 1 cm/½ in headspace for expansion. Alternatively you can open freeze on trays before packing into bags or boxes. Seal, label and store for up to 12 months.

Blanching and Cooking Vegetables

Type per 450 g/1 lb	Blanching time on High	Microwaving time on High	Special Instructions
Beans, green	2-3 mins	5-7 mins	Use 75ml/5tbsp water. Add a pinch of salt
Broccoli florets	2-3 mins	7-8 mins	Use 75 ml/5tbsp water. Add a pinch of salt
Brussel sprouts, whole	3 mins	6-8 mins	
Carrots, slices	3 mins	8-10 mins	
Cauliflower florets	2 ½ mins	8-10 mins	Use 75 ml/5tbsp water
Courgettes, slices	1 ½ mins	8-10 mins	No water
Greens, spinach	1 ½ mins	8-10 mins	
Peas, whole	2 mins	8-10 mins	

OATMEAL AUBERGINE

Serves 6

Ingredients	Metric	Imperial	American
Large aubergine, peeled and sliced	450g	1 lb	1 lb
Water, hot	750 ml	1 ¼ pts	3 cups
Salt	15 ml	1 tbsp	1 tbsp
Butter or margarine	30 ml	2 tbsp	2 tbsp
Egg, beaten	1	1	1
Dry breadcrumbs	100 g	4 oz	1 cup
Oatmeal	50 g	2 oz	½ cup

Soak the aubergine in salted water for 5 minutes then drain.

Melt the butter or margarine in a shallow dish on High for 30-45 seconds. Mix in the egg. In another shallow dish, mix the breadcrumbs and oatmeal. Dip the aubergine slices in the egg mixture, then coat with crumbs. Arrange half the slices around the edge of a baking sheet and microwave on High for 8-10 minutes until just tender. Repeat with remaining slices.

To Freeze: Open freeze on paper-lined trays until firm then pack and freeze for up to 2 months.

To Serve: Arrange the slices in batches on a baking sheet and microwave on High for 8-10 minutes.

STUFFED CABBAGE IN TOMATO SAUCE

Serves 4 – 6

Ingredients	Metric	Imperial	American
Cabbage leaves	*8*	*8*	*8*
Onion, chopped	*1*	*1*	*1*
Oil	*15 ml*	*1 tbsp*	*1 tbsp*
Minced (ground) beef	*450 g*	*1 lb*	*1 lb*
Canned tomatoes	*400 g*	*14 oz*	*14 oz*
Cornflour (cornstarch)	*10 ml*	*2 tsp*	*2 tsp*
Worcestershire sauce	*15 ml*	*1 tbsp*	*1 tbsp*
Dried mixed herbs	*2.5 ml*	*1/2 tsp*	*1/2 tsp*
Chopped fresh parsley	*15 ml*	*1 tbsp*	*1 tbsp*
Salt and pepper			
For The Sauce			
Tomato purée (paste)	*15 ml*	*1 tbsp*	*1 tbsp*
Cornflour (cornstarch)	*10 ml*	*2 tsp*	*2 tsp*
Worcestershire sauce	*5 ml*	*1 tsp*	*1 tsp*
Sugar	*2.5 ml*	*1/2 tsp*	*1/2 tsp*

Put the cabbage leaves into a large bowl, cover with 1.8l/3 pts/7 1/2 cups hot water and microwave on High for 3 minutes. Drain well. Place the onion in a bowl with the oil and microwave on High for 2 minutes. Stir in the beef. Drain the tomatoes, reserving the juice. Add the tomatoes to the meat with the cornflour, Worcestershire sauce, herbs, parsley, salt and pepper and microwave on High for 6-7 minutes, stirring twice. Put the cabbage leaves flat on a board and divide the stuffing between them. Roll up the cabbage leaves, folding in the sides to form neat parcels. Place in a serving dish and keep on one side.

To make the sauce, put the juice from the tomatoes into a jug. Stir in the tomato purée and make up to 300ml/ 1/2 pt/ 1 1/4 cups with water. Mix the cornflour with a little of this liquid and add with the Worcestershire sauce, sugar, salt and pepper. Microwave on High for 3-4 minutes, stirring twice. Pour over the stuffed cabbage leaves and microwave on High for 2 minutes.

To Freeze: Freeze in a rigid container for up to 2 months.

To Serve: Microwave on High for 15 minutes, stirring occasionally.

STUFFED COURGETTES

Serves 4 – 6

Ingredients	Metric	Imperial	American
Courgettes	*4*	*4*	*4*
Green or red pepper, chopped	*1*	*1*	*1*
Celery stick, chopped	*1*	*1*	*1*
Onion, chopped	*1*	*1*	*1*
Garlic clove, chopped	*1*	*1*	*1*
Butter or margarine	*15 ml*	*1 tbsp*	*1 tbsp*
Quick-cook long-grain rice	*100 g*	*4 oz*	*1/2 cup*
Tomato sauce (see page 148)	*300 ml*	*1/2 pt*	*1 1/4 cups*
Water	*60 ml*	*4 tbsp*	*4 tbsp*
Chopped fresh parsley	*15 ml*	*1 tbsp*	*1 tbsp*
Paprika	*2.5 ml*	*1/2 tsp*	*1/2 tsp*
Salt and pepper			
Worcestershire sauce	*2.5 ml*	*1/2 tsp*	*1/2 tsp*
To Garnish			
Soured cream	*60 ml*	*4 tbsp*	*4 tbsp*
Black olives, stoned and chopped	*12*	*12*	*12*

Halve the courgettes lengthways and scoop out the pulp, leaving a 5 mm/¹/₄ in shell. Chop the pulp coarsely and set aside. Arrange the courgette shells cut side up on a baking sheet. Cover with plastic wrap and microwave on High for 4 minutes until very hot.

Put the courgette flesh, pepper, celery, onion, garlic and butter or margarine into a casserole dish, cover and microwave on High for 5-6 minutes until tender, stirring once. Stir in the remaining ingredients, cover and microwave on High for 5-7 minutes until the liquid is absorbed and the rice is tender. Spoon the stuffing into the courgette shells. Garnish each courgette half with soured cream and chopped olives.

To Freeze: Open freeze without the garnish until firm. Wrap, label and freeze for up to 2 months.

To Serve: Thaw in 2 batches, covered with waxed paper. Microwave on High for 5-10 minutes until hot, rearranging the shells once. Leave to stand, covered, for 5 minutes.

LEEKS A LA GRECQUE

Serves 6

Ingredients	Metric	Imperial	American
Leeks	*6*	*6*	*6*
Vegetable oil	*15 ml*	*1 tbsp*	*1 tbsp*
Onion, chopped	*1*	*1*	*1*
Garlic cloves, chopped	*2*	*2*	*2*
Mushrooms, sliced	*100 g*	*4 oz*	*1/4 lb*
Canned tomatoes, sieved	*400 g*	*14 oz*	*14 oz*
Tomato purée (paste)	*30 ml*	*2 tbsp*	*2 tbsp*
Mustard	*5 ml*	*1 tsp*	*1 tsp*
Salt and pepper			

Slice the leeks in half lengthways and clean thoroughly, discarding the outside leaves. Place in a glass bowl, sprinkle with water and microwave on High for 8-9 minutes. Cool. Place the oil in a bowl and add the onion, garlic and mushrooms. Microwave on High for 3-4 minutes.

Mix the tomatoes, tomato purée and seasonings. Add to the onion mixture and stir thoroughly. Cover with a lid or plate, leaving a gap to allow steam to escape. Microwave on High for 8-9 minutes. Cool. Serve the cold leeks with the cold sauce and hot French bread.

To Freeze: Freeze for up to 2 months

To Serve: Microwave on High for 10-14 minutes.

ONION AND PARSNIP BAKE

Serves 4

Ingredients	Metric	Imperial	American
Onions, sliced	*225 g*	*8 oz*	*¹/₂ lb*
Parsnips, sliced	*225 g*	*8 oz*	*¹/₂ lb*
Salt and pepper			
Chopped fresh parsley	*15 ml*	*1 tbsp*	*1 tbsp*
White wine	*45 ml*	*3 tbsp*	*3 tbsp*
Plain flour	*25 g*	*1 oz*	*¹/₄ cup*
Milk	*300 ml*	*¹/₂ pt*	*1 ¹/₄ cups*
Butter or margarine	*15 ml*	*1 tbsp*	*1 tbsp*
Egg, beaten	*1*	*1*	*1*

Arrange half the onions in the base of a shallow flameproof casserole dish with half the parsnips on top. Season with half the parsley and salt and pepper. Repeat with the remaining onions, parsnips and parsley. Pour over the wine, cover and cook on High for 6-7 minutes. Leave to stand while you make the topping.

Mix the flour to a paste with a little milk then stir in the remaining milk and season with salt and pepper. Dot the butter or margarine on top and microwave on High for 2-3 minutes, stir well then cook for a further 1¹/₂ minutes. Leave to stand for 1 minute. Stir in the egg and pour over the vegetables. Brown the dish under a conventional grill.

To Freeze: Cool and freeze in the container for up to 2 months.

To Serve: Thaw on Defrost or Low for 10 minutes, stand for 10 minutes, then reheat on High for 8 minutes. Brown under a grill.

STUFFED BAKED POTATOES

Serves 4

Ingredients	Metric	Imperial	American
Large potatoes	*4*	*4*	*4*
Various fillings (see opposite)			
Cheddar cheese, grated	*25 g*	*1 oz*	*¹/₄ cup*

Scrub the potatoes well and prick the skins all over with a fork. Microwave on High for 8 minutes. Turn the potatoes and continue cooking for 6 minutes. Take out of the oven and leave to stand for 5 minutes. Cut the top from each potato and scoop out the potato flesh into a bowl, leaving a 'wall' of flesh and potato skin. Mix the potato with chosen filling and refill the potatoes. Sprinkle with cheese and microwave on High for 3 minutes.

FILLINGS

Minced Beef – While the potatoes are standing, microwave 225 g/8 oz/ ¹/₂ lb minced (ground) beef and 1 small onion, chopped finely, for 4 minutes. Mix with the potato with 1 tblsp tomato ketchup, salt and pepper.

Smoked Fish – Cut the corner of a boil-in-the-bag containing 150 g/ 6 oz/ 6 oz smoked haddock. Put the bag on a plate and microwave on High for 5 minutes. Remove any skin from the fish and break the flesh into flakes. Mix fish with the potato, 50 g/2 oz/ ¹/₄ cup butter or margarine, salt and pepper.

Ham and Cheese – Mix 100 g/4 oz/1 cup finely chopped cooked ham with 50 g/ 2 oz/ ¹/₂ cup grated Cheddar cheese, 25 g/ 1 oz/ 2 tbsp butter, 2 tsp Worcestershire sauce, salt and pepper. Mix with the potato.

To Freeze: Wrap individually before assembling and freeze for up to 1 month.

To Serve: Microwave on High for 5 minutes for each potato.

RATATOUILLE

Serves 4 – 6

Ingredients	Metric	Imperial	American
Aubergine, sliced	*1*	*1*	*1*
Salt			
Courgettes, sliced	*2*	*2*	*2*
Onion, sliced	*1*	*1*	*1*
Green pepper, chopped	*1*	*1*	*1*
Red pepper, chopped	*1*	*1*	*1*
Garlic clove, crushed	*1*	*1*	*1*
Olive oil	*15 ml*	*1 tbsp*	*1 tbsp*
Tomato sauce (see page 148)	*300 ml*	*1/2 pt*	*1 1/4 cups*
Dried oregano	*2.5 ml*	*1/2 tsp*	*1/2 tsp*
Black pepper			

Soak the aubergine in salted water for 5 minutes then drain. Place in a bowl and microwave on High for 4-5 minutes. Drain.

Put the courgettes in a casserole dish, cover and microwave on High for 2-4 minutes until tender, stirring once or twice. Drain. Arrange the courgettes and aubergines in overlapping layers along the sides and bottom of a pie plate.

In a medium-sized bowl combine the onion, peppers, garlic and olive oil, cover and microwave on High for 3-5 minutes until tender. Drain. Stir in tomato sauce, oregano and pepper. Spoon over the courgettes. Microwave on High for 7-10 minutes until hot. Leave to stand for 2 minutes. Not suitable for freezing.

SWEET AND SOUR BEETROOT

Serves 4

Ingredients	Metric	Imperial	American
Beetroot	*450 g*	*1 lb*	*1 lb*
Salt	*2.5 ml*	*1/2 tsp*	*1/2 tsp*
Hot water	*120 ml*	*4 fl oz*	*1/2 cup*
Butter or margarine	*15 ml*	*1 tbsp*	*1 tbsp*
Soft brown sugar	*15 ml*	*1 tbsp*	*1 tbsp*
White wine vinegar	*15 ml*	*1 tbsp*	*1 tbsp*
Soured cream	*15 ml*	*1 tbsp*	*1 tbsp*

Leave root ends and 5 cm/2 in tops on the beetroot, clean and place in a casserole. Dissolve the salt in the water then pour over the beetroots, cover and microwave on High for 14-16 minutes until tender, stirring once or twice. Leave to stand for 3-4 minutes. Remove the skins and tops, trim the root ends and slice.

Put the butter or margarine into a small bowl and microwave on High for 30-45 seconds until melted. Stir in the sugar and wine vinegar, and microwave on High for 1-2 minutes until the sugar dissolves, stirring once. Pour the sauce over the beetroot. Garnish with the soured cream.

To Freeze: Freeze in a rigid container for up to 1 month.

To Serve: Transfer to a casserole dish, cover and microwave on High for 7-10 minutes until hot, stirring and separating the beetroot slices once or twice.

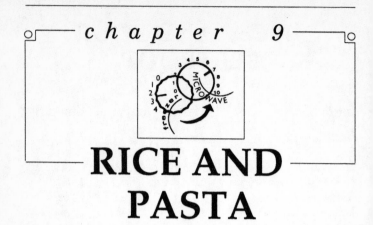

chapter 9

RICE AND PASTA

Rice cooked in the microwave and stored in the freezer can complete a meal at a moment's notice.

RICE

Serves 4

Ingredients	Metric	Imperial	American
Hot water	*600 ml*	*1 ¼ pts*	*2 ½ cups*
Long-grain rice	*225 g*	*8 oz*	*1 cup*
Butter or margarine	*15 ml*	*1 tbsp*	*1 tbsp*
Salt	*5 ml*	*1 tsp*	*1 tsp*

Combine all the ingredients in a casserole dish, cover and microwave on High for 5 minutes. Reduce the power to Medium and microwave for 14-17 minutes until the liquid is absorbed and the rice is tender. Leave to stand for 5 minutes, then fluff up with a fork.

To Freeze: Freeze in rigid containers for up to 1 month.

To Serve: Transfer to a casserole dish, cover and microwave on High for 4-8 minutes until hot, breaking apart and stirring 2 or 3 times.

Variation: If you use brown rice, increase the cooking time on Medium to 30-35 minutes.

CHICKEN AND VEGETABLE RICE

Serves 4

Ingredients	Metric	Imperial	American
Celery stick, sliced	*1*	*1*	*1*
Button mushrooms,			
sliced	*100 g*	*4 oz*	*4 oz*
Carrot, finely chopped	*1*	*1*	*1*
Small red pepper,			
chopped	*1*	*1*	*1*
Small onion, chopped	*1*	*1*	*1*
Garlic clove, crushed	*1*	*1*	*1*
Butter or margarine	*30 ml*	*2 tbsp*	*2 tbsp*
Cooked brown or			
white rice			
(see page 122)			
Cooked chicken, cubed	*100 g*	*4 oz*	*¹/₄ lb*
Salt and pepper			

Put the vegetables and butter or margarine into a
casserole dish, cover and microwave on High for 4-5
minutes until the vegetables are tender, stirring once or
twice. Stir in the rice, chicken, salt and pepper, cover
and microwave on High for 2-3 minutes until heated
through.

To Freeze: Freeze before the final cooking for up to 1
month.

To Serve: Transfer to a casserole dish, cover and
microwave on High for 1-2 minutes until defrosted,
stirring once. Continue to microwave, covered, on High
for 2-4 minutes until heated, stirring once.

FRIED RICE

Serves 4 – 6

Ingredients	Metric	Imperial	American
Chicken and Vegetable *Rice (see page 123),* *defrosted*	*1*	*1*	*1*
Eggs, lightly beaten	*2*	*2*	*2*
Butter or margarine	*15 ml*	*1 tbsp*	*1 tbsp*
Soy sauce	*30 ml*	*2 tbsp*	*2 tbsp*

Put the Chicken and Vegetable Rice into a casserole dish, cover and microwave on High for 4-6 minutes until heated, stirring twice.

Put the beaten eggs and butter into a small bowl and microwave on High for 1-2 minutes until the eggs are set, stirring once. Cut the eggs into slivers and stir into the rice with the soy sauce, tossing to coat the rice.

ITALIAN RISOTTO

Serves 8

Ingredients	Metric	Imperial	American
Long-grain rice	*225 g*	*8 oz*	*1 cup*
Onions, chopped	*2*	*2*	*2*
Garlic cloves, chopped	*2*	*2*	*2*
Vegetable oil	*15 ml*	*1 tbsp*	*1 tbsp*
Celery stick, chopped	*1*	*1*	*1*
Mushrooms, sliced	*50 g*	*2 oz*	*2 oz*
Canned tomatoes, sieved	*400 g*	*14 oz*	*14 oz*
Tomato purée (paste)	*30 ml*	*2 tbsp*	*2 tbsp*
Water	*30 ml*	*2 tbsp*	*2 tbsp*
Salt and pepper			
Dried basil	*5 ml*	*1 tsp*	*1 tsp*
Pine nuts	*30 ml*	*2 tbsp*	*2 tbsp*
Grated Parmesan cheese	*30 ml*	*2 tbsp*	*2 tbsp*

To Garnish
Chopped fresh parsley

Place the rice in a casserole dish. Place the onion and garlic in a bowl and sprinkle on the oil. Microwave on High for 3 minutes. Add the celery and mushrooms. Microwave on High for a further 3 minutes. Add the tomatoes, tomato purée, water and seasonings and add to the rice with the vegetables. Stir thoroughly. Sprinkle the pine nuts and Parmesan cheese on top. Microwave on High for 20-23 minutes. Leave to stand for 5 minutes. Serve garnished with parsley.

To Freeze: Freeze for up to 2 months.

To Serve: Microwave on High for 6-8 minutes, stirring occasionally.

CURRIED RICE

Serves 4 – 6

Ingredients	Metric	Imperial	American
Small apple, peeled, cored and chopped	1	1	1
Butter or margarine	15 ml	1 tbsp	1 tbsp
Chicken and Vegetable Rice (see page 123), defrosted	1	1	1
Sultanas	50 g	2 oz	1/3 cup
Curry powder	10 ml	2 tsp	2 tsp

Put the apple and butter or margarine into a small bowl and microwave on High for 2-3 minutes until the apple is tender.

Put the chicken and vegetable rice, apple, sultanas and curry powder into a casserole dish, cover and microwave on High for 5-7 minutes until heated, stirring twice.

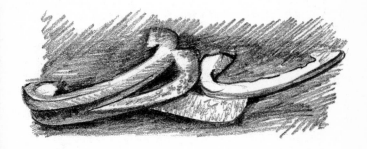

MACARONI CHEESE

Serves 4

Ingredients	Metric	Imperial	American
Macaroni	*225 g*	*8 oz*	*¹/₂ lb*
Boiling water	*1.2 lt*	*2 pts*	*5 cups*
Salt	*5 ml*	*1 tsp*	*1 tsp*
Butter or margarine	*50 g*	*2 oz*	*¹/₄ cup*
Onion, chopped	*1*	*1*	*1*
Bacon rashers, chopped	*2*	*2*	*2*
Plain flour	*25 g*	*1 oz*	*2 tbsp*
Milk	*600 ml*	*1 pt*	*2 ¹/₂ cups*
Cheddar cheese, grated	*175 g*	*6 oz*	*6 oz*
Salt and pepper			
Pinch of paprika			

Put the macaroni into a large bowl and add the hot water and salt. Microwave on High for 13-15 minutes, stirring twice. Put the butter or margarine into a bowl and microwave on High for 1 minute. Add the onion and bacon and microwave on High for 4 minutes. Stir in the flour and add the milk gradually. Microwave on High for 5 minutes, stirring twice. Stir in the cheese and leave to stand for 2 minutes. Stir in the macaroni and season. Microwave for 4 minutes, stirring 4 times. Sprinkle with paprika before serving.

To Freeze: Freeze for up to 2 months.

To Serve: Microwave on High for 10 minutes, stirring occasionally.

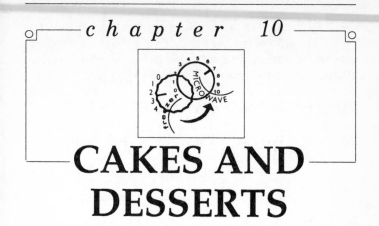

CAKES AND DESSERTS

Using the microwave oven and freezer means you can quickly serve attractive desserts for entertaining or family meals. Even when frozen, cakes and pies are delicate. Choose a place in the freezer where they will not be damaged by contact with hard or sharp objects.

PACKING FOR THE FREEZER

Iced cakes should be frozen until firm before wrapping to avoid spoiling the icing. Wrap in plastic wrap, then overwrap with heavy-duty foil. Cakes that are not iced should be wrapped as soon as they are cool to prevent them from drying out.

Use glass or ovenproof paper pie plates to prepare, freeze and defrost pies. Leave the pie in the pie plate and place in the freezer until firm. Wrap the pie and the plate in heavy-duty foil.

Freeze moulded desserts such as mousses in

their dishes, wrapped securely with heavy-duty foil. To serve, unwrap and dip briefly in hot water. Loosen the edges of the mould with a knife, and then invert on to a serving plate.

THAWING CAKES AND DESSERTS

Item	Weight	Thawing time on Medium-Low	Procedure
Layer cakes with icing	275-450 g/ 10-16 oz 450-550 g/ 1-1 $^{1}/_{4}$ lb 550-800 g/ 1 $^{1}/_{4}$-1 $^{3}/_{4}$ lb	1-3 $^{1}/_{2}$ mins 1 $^{1}/_{2}$-4 mins 3 $^{1}/_{2}$-6 mins	Remove from package and transfer to serving plate. Thaw until wooden pick can be easily inserted in the centre, rotating 2 or 3 times. Leave to stand 15-20 minutes.
Fruit cakes	275-400 g/ 10-14 oz 400-450 g/ 14-16 oz	$^{3}/_{4}$-1 $^{1}/_{2}$ mins 1-2 mins	Remove from package and transfer to serving plate. Thaw until wooden pick can be easily inserted in the centre, rotating 2 or 3 times. Leave to stand 5 minutes.
Cheesecakes	275-450 g/ 10-16 oz 450-550 g/ 1-1 $^{1}/_{4}$ lb	1-3 $^{1}/_{2}$ mins 1 $^{1}/_{2}$-4 mins	Remove from package and transfer to serving plate. Thaw until wooden pick can be easily inserted in the centre, rotating 2 or 3 times. Leave to stand 10-15 minutes.

BREAD PUDDING

Serves 4 – 6

Ingredients	Metric	Imperial	American
Soft brown sugar	100 g	4 oz	1/2 cup
Cornflour (cornstarch)	30 ml	2 tbsp	2 tbsp
Pinch of salt			
Milk	375 ml	13 fl oz	1 1/2 cups
Eggs	3	3	3
Wholewheat bread, cubed	225 g	8 oz	1/2 lb
Sultanas (golden raisins)	100 g	4 oz	2/3 cup
Ground cinnamon	2.5 ml	1/2 tsp	1/2 tsp
Pinch of grated nutmeg			

Line a casserole dish with foil. In a medium-sized bowl blend the sugar, cornflour, salt, milk and eggs. In the prepared casserole combine the bread cubes, sultanas, cinnamon and nutmeg, tossing to coat. Pour the milk mixture on top. Gently press down. Microwave on Medium for 15-20 minutes then leave to stand for 10 minutes.

To Freeze: Before cooking, freeze until firm. Remove from casserole with foil liner. Wrap, label, and freeze for up to 1 month.

To Serve: Unwrap and place in a casserole dish. Cover with waxed paper. Microwave on Medium for 25-35 minutes, or until soft set in the centre, gently breaking up and pushing the edges towards the centre with a rubber spatula once or twice. Leave to stand for 10 minutes.

APPLE AND APRICOT SPONGE

Serves 4

Ingredients	Metric	Imperial	American
Eating apples, peeled, cored and sliced	*450 g*	*1 lb*	*1 lb*
Canned apricots, drained	*225 g*	*8 oz*	*¹/₂ lb*
Butter or margarine	*50 g*	*2 oz*	*¹/₄ cup*
Caster sugar	*50 g*	*2 oz*	*¹/₄ cup*
Egg	*1*	*1*	*1*
Self-raising flour	*50 g*	*2 oz*	*¹/₂ cup*
Chopped walnuts	*50 g*	*¹/₂ cup*	*2 oz*

Put the apples in a pie dish with the apricots and spoon on 45 ml/3 tbsp of syrup from the can. Microwave on High for 4-5 minutes. Cream the margarine and sugar until light and fluffy. Work in the egg and fold in the flour and walnuts. Spread over the fruit. Microwave on High for 5-6 minutes. Leave to stand for 3 minutes and serve with cream or ice cream.

To Freeze: Freeze for up to 2 months.

To Serve: Microwave on High for 10 minutes.

NUT CAKE

Makes 1 x 20 cm/8 in cake

Ingredients	Metric	Imperial	American
Plain flour	*150g*	*5 oz*	*1 1/4 cups*
Pinch of salt			
Ground cinnamon	*2.5 ml*	*1/2 tsp*	*1/2 tsp*
Soft brown sugar	*75 g*	*3 oz*	*1/2 cup*
Caster sugar	*75 g*	*3 oz*	*1/3 cup*
Vegetable oil	*75 ml*	*5 tbsp*	*5 tbsp*
Walnuts, chopped	*25 g*	*1 oz*	*1/4 cup*
Baking powder	*5 ml*	*1 tsp*	*1 tsp*
Bicarbonate of soda			
(baking soda)	*2.5 ml*	*1/2 tsp*	*1/2 tsp*
Egg	*1*	*1*	*1*
Milk	*150 ml*	*1/4 pt*	*2/3 cup*

Sift the flour, salt and half the cinnamon together. Add the brown and white sugars and the oil and beat until well mixed. Take 6 tablespoons of this mixture and mix with the nuts and the remaining cinnamon. Add the baking powder, soda, egg and milk to the remaining mixture and beat until smooth. Put this mixture into a 20 cm/8 in greased round cake dish and sprinkle on the nut mixture. Microwave on High for 8 minutes. Leave to stand for 10 minutes and serve warm.

To Freeze: Freeze for up to 2 months.

To Serve: Microwave on Medium for 4-5 minutes.

APPLESAUCE CAKE

Makes 1

Ingredients	Metric	Imperial	American
Plain flour	*175 g*	*6 oz*	*1 1/2 cups*
Baking powder	*2.5 ml*	*1/2 tsp*	*1/2 tsp*
Salt	*2.5 ml*	*1/2 tsp*	*1/2 tsp*
Pinch of ground cloves			
Pinch of ground nutmeg			
Pinch of ground all-spice			
Butter or margarine	*100 g*	*4 oz*	*1/2 cup*
Soft brown sugar	*175 g*	*6 oz*	*1 cup*
Egg	*1*	*1*	*1*
Unsweetened applesauce	*300 ml*	*1/2 pt*	*1 1/4 cups*
Sultanas	*50 g*	*2 oz*	*1/3 cup*

Lightly grease and flour a shallow square baking dish.
Sift together the flour, baking powder, salt and spices.
Cream the fat and sugar together until light and fluffy.
Work in the egg. Mix the applesauce and sultanas
together. Add the dry ingredients and the apple mixture
alternately to the creamed mixture and beat well. Pour
into the baking dish. Microwave on High for 10-12
minutes and cool in the dish before cutting into squares.

To Freeze: Before cutting into squares, freeze in the
dish for up to 2 months.

To Serve: Thaw at room temperature for 3 hours.

CHOCOLATE CHIP CAKE

Makes 1 x 20 cm/8 in cake

Ingredients	Metric	Imperial	American
Self-raising flour	*100 g*	*4 oz*	*1 cup*
Cocoa powder	*50 g*	*2 oz*	*1/2 cup*
Chocolate chips	*100 g*	*4 oz*	*1/4 lb*
Butter or margarine, softened	*100 g*	*4 oz*	*1/2 cup*
Caster sugar	*100g*	*4 oz*	*1/2 cup*
Eggs, beaten	*2*	*2*	*2*
Milk	*30- 45 ml*	*2- 3 tbsp*	*2- 3 tbsp*

Beat together all the ingredients until smooth, adding the milk gradually to obtain a light consistency. Pour into a lined cake dish and microwave on Medium for 5-6 minutes. Leave to stand for 5 minutes then turn out and serve with cream.

To Freeze: Freeze for up to 2 months.

To Serve: Microwave on Medium for 3-4 minutes.

GINGER CAKE

Makes 1 x 20 cm/8 in cake

Ingredients	Metric	Imperial	American
Golden syrup	*350 g*	*12 oz*	*12 oz*
Butter or margarine	*150 g*	*5 oz*	*²/₃ cup*
Plain flour	*250 g*	*9 oz*	*1 ¹/₄ cups*
Pinch of salt			
Bicarbonate of soda			
(baking soda)	*10 ml*	*2 tsp*	*2 tsp*
Ground ginger	*10 ml*	*2 tsp*	*2 tsp*
Egg, beaten	*1*	*1*	*1*
Milk	*300 ml*	*¹/₂ pt*	*1 ¹/₄ cups*
Icing sugar			
(confectioners, sugar)	*30 ml*	*2 tbsp*	*2 tbsp*

Microwave the syrup and butter or margarine on High for 2 minutes. Mix the dry ingredients together in a bowl then pour in the melted syrup and butter and stir until well mixed. Stir in the egg and milk. Pour into a lined cake tin and microwave on Low for 18-20 minutes. Leave to stand for 5 minutes then turn out and leave to cool. Wrap in foil and store for 2 days before serving. Serve dusted with icing sugar.

To Freeze: Freeze for up to 2 months.

To Serve: Thaw on Defrost or Low for 4-6 minutes, leave to stand for 5 minutes.

FRUIT CAKE

Makes 1 x 18 cm/7 in cake

Ingredients	Metric	Imperial	American
Butter or margarine,			
softened	*100g*	*4 oz*	*$1/2$ cup*
Self-raising flour	*225 g*	*8 oz*	*2 cups*
Soft brown sugar	*100g*	*4 oz*	*$1/2$ cup*
Mixed fruit	*175 g*	*6 oz*	*1 cup*
Eggs, beaten	*2*	*2*	*2*
Golden syrup	*15 ml*	*1 tbsp*	*1 tbsp*
Milk	*30 ml*	*2 tbsp*	*2 tbsp*

Rub the butter or margarine into the flour until the mixture resembles breadcrumbs. Stir in the sugar and fruit. Beat the eggs, syrup and milk together then mix into the dry ingredients. Pour into a lined cake dish and microwave on Medium for 5-6 minutes. Cool on a wire rack.

To Freeze: Freeze for up to 2 months.

To Serve: Microwave on Medium for 4-5 minutes.

CHOCOLATE CHIP BISCUITS

Makes 4 dozen

Ingredients	Metric	Imperial	American
Soft brown sugar	350 g	12 oz	1 ¹/₂ cups
Bicarbonate of soda (baking soda)	7.5 ml	1 ¹/₂ tsp	1 ¹/₂ tsp
Salt	2.5 ml	¹/₂ tsp	¹/₂ tsp
Butter or margarine	175 g	6 oz	³/₄ cup
Eggs	2	2	2
Vanilla essence (extract)	7.5 ml	1 ¹/₂ tsp	1 ¹/₂ tsp
Plain flour	450 g	1 lb	4 cups
Wholewheat flour	350 g	12 oz	3 cups
Plain chocolate chips	150 g	6 oz	6 oz

In a large bowl mix the brown sugar, baking soda, salt, butter, eggs and vanilla essence until light and fluffy. Stir in the remaining ingredients. Divide the dough into four equal parts. Shape each part into a roll 15 cm/6 in long. Cut the rolls into 2.5 cm/1 in slices and halve each slice. Arrange four halves on a baking sheet lined with waxed paper and microwave on Medium for 1-3 minutes until just dry on the surface.

To Freeze: Before baking freeze the dough for up to 3 months.

To Serve: Unwrap and slice the dough, then continue with the recipe.

TRUFFLES

Makes 3 – 4 dozen

Ingredients	Metric	Imperial	American
Milk chocolate	*350 g*	*12 oz*	*12 oz*
Butter or margarine,			
cut into pieces	*150 g*	*6 oz*	*³/₄ cup*
Eggs, beaten	*2*	*2*	*2*
Egg yolks, beaten	*2*	*2*	*2*
Ground hazelnuts	*200 g*	*7 oz*	*1 ³/₄ cups*
Crème de menthe	*75 ml*	*5 tbsp*	*5 tbsp*
Cocoa powder	*30 ml*	*2 tbsp*	*2 tbsp*

Put the chocolate into a medium-sized bowl and microwave on Medium for 2-4 minutes until melted, stirring 2 or 3 times. Stir in the butter or margarine until melted. Blend in the eggs and egg yolks. Microwave on Medium for 4-5 minutes until very hot and thick, whisking several times. Blend in half the ground hazelnuts and the crème de menthe. Refrigerate for 3 hours or until the mixture is firm enough to shape into balls. Shape into 2.5 cm/1 in balls.

Mix the remaining ground hazelnuts with the cocoa. Roll the balls in this mixture to coat.

To Freeze: Open freeze in a single layer until firm, then wrap, label and freeze for up to 6 months.

To Serve: Thaw on Defrost or Low in batches of 12 for 1 minute, rearranging once.

FUDGE

Makes 1.5 kg/3 lb

Ingredients	Metric	Imperial	American
Sugar	450 g	1 lb	2 cups
Bicarbonate of soda (baking soda)	5 ml	1 tsp	1 tsp
Evaporated milk	250 ml	8 fl oz	1 cup
Butter or margarine	150 g	6 oz	3/4 cup
Vanilla essence (extract)	5 ml	1 tsp	1 tsp
Milk chocolate chips	100 g	4 oz	1/4 lb
Pecan nuts, coarsely broken	225 g	8 oz	2 cups

Put the sugar, bicarbonate of soda, evaporated milk and butter or margarine into a bowl and microwave on Medium-High for 20-25 minutes, or until syrup dropped into very cold water forms a soft ball which flattens on removal from the water. Stir several times during cooking.

Add the vanilla essence and beat with an electric mixer on high speed for 2 minutes, scraping the bowl occasionally. Add the chocolate chips. Beat with the electric mixer until the chips melt. Stir in the nuts. Press the mixture into a foil lined 23 cm/9 in baking dish and refrigerate until set.

Remove from the dish with the foil lining. Cut into serving pieces, but do not separate. Divide into three 450 g/ 1 lb sections.

To Freeze: Freeze for up to 6 months.

To Serve: Thaw one-third at a time on Medium-Low for 2 minutes, rearranging every 30 seconds. Leave to stand for 9-10 minutes.

c h a p t e r   11

SAUCES

Sauces freeze well and can be made in advance
and frozen in quantities suitable for your own
requirements.

PACKING FOR THE FREEZER
Pour sauces into rigid containers, allowing a
little head room for expansion. Cool, cover, label
and freeze. You can also freeze sauces in freezer
bags, shaped by placing them in a margarine tub.

THAWING AND REHEATING
Transfer sauces to a casserole dish, cover and
reheat on High, stirring regularly.

TOMATO SAUCE

Serves 4 – 6

Ingredients	Metric	Imperial	American
Tomatoes, skinned, seeded and puréed	*12*	*12*	*12*
Tomato purée (paste)	*350 g*	*12 oz*	*12 oz*
Small green pepper, chopped	*1*	*1*	*1*
Small onion, chopped	*1*	*1*	*1*
Olive oil	*15 ml*	*1 tbsp*	*1 tbsp*
Sugar	*10 ml*	*2 tsp*	*2 tsp*
Salt	*5 ml*	*1 tsp*	*1 tsp*
Dried basil	*5 ml*	*1/2 tsp*	*1/2 tsp*
Black pepper			
Bay leaf, crumbled	*1*	*1*	*1*

Put all the ingredients into a casserole, cover and microwave on High for 10 minutes. Stir. Microwave, uncovered, on High, for 35-45 minutes until the sauce is thick, stirring several times.

To Freeze: Freeze in several rigid containers for up to 3 months.

To Serve: Transfer the sauce from one container into a small bowl and microwave on High for 3-4 minutes, breaking apart and stirring several times.

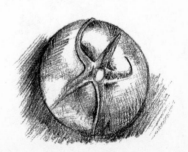

MUSTARD SAUCE

Serves 4

Ingredients	Metric	Imperial	American
Butter or margarine	*30 ml*	*2 tbsp*	*2 tbsp*
Plain flour	*30 ml*	*2 tbsp*	*2 tbsp*
Milk	*250 ml*	*8 fl oz*	*1 cup*
Dijon mustard	*15 ml*	*1 tbsp*	*1 tbsp*
Pinch of mustard powder			
Egg yolk, lightly beaten	*1*	*1*	*1*
Chopped fresh parsley	*15 ml*	*1 tbsp*	*1 tbsp*
Red wine vinegar	*2.5 ml*	*¹/₂ tsp*	*¹/₂ tsp*

Put the butter or margarine into a bowl and microwave on High for 30-45 seconds until melted. Stir in the flour, milk and mustards and microwave on Medium for 5-6 minutes until thickened, stirring several times. Stir a little of the hot mixture into the beaten egg yolk. Return this to the hot mixture, stirring constantly. Mix in the remaining ingredients. Microwave on Medium for 1 minute and stir well before serving. Serve with ham dishes.

To Freeze: Freeze in a rigid container for up to 1 month.

To Serve: Microwave on Medium for 10-12 minutes stirring occasionally.

BACON AND TOMATO SAUCE

Serves 4

Ingredients	Metric	Imperial	American
Onions, chopped	*2*	*2*	*2*
Bacon rashers, chopped	*2*	*2*	*2*
Canned tomatoes	*400 g*	*14 oz*	*14 oz*
Tomato purée (paste)	*45 ml*	*3 tbsp*	*3 tbsp*
Olive oil	*15 ml*	*1 tbsp*	*1 tbsp*
Red wine	*15 ml*	*1 tbsp*	*1 tbsp*
Garlic clove, crushed	*1*	*1*	*1*
Bay leaf, crumbled	*1*	*1*	*1*
Brown sugar	*10 ml*	*2 tsp*	*2 tsp*
Salt and pepper			

Put the onions and bacon into a casserole, cover and microwave on High for 2-3 minutes until the onion is tender, stirring once. Stir in the remaining ingredients and microwave on Medium for 10-15 minutes until the flavours blend and the sauce is of the desired consis--tency, stirring 2 or 3 times. Serve with spaghetti, meatballs or grilled meats.

To Freeze: Freeze in a rigid container for up to 2 months.

To Serve: Microwave on High for 10-12 minutes, stirring occasionally.

SWEET AND SOUR SAUCE

Serves 4

Ingredients	Metric	Imperial	American
White wine vinegar	*60 ml*	*4 tbsp*	*4 tbsp*
Cornflour (cornstarch)	*15 ml*	*1 tbsp*	*1 tbsp*
Canned pineapple,			
drained and crushed	*400 g*	*14 oz*	*14 oz*
Apricot jam	*100 g*	*4 oz*	*¼ lb*
Green pepper, chopped	*1*	*1*	*1*
Brown sugar	*50 g*	*2 oz*	*¼ cup*
Soy sauce	*15 ml*	*1 tbsp*	*1 tbsp*
Ground ginger	*2.5 ml*	*½ tsp*	*½ tsp*

Blend the wine vinegar and cornflour and stir in the remaining ingredients. Microwave on High for 6-8 minutes until the mixture is clear and thick, stirring several times. Serve with rice and pork or chicken.

To Freeze: Freeze in a rigid container for up to 2 months.

To Serve: Microwave on High for 12-15 minutes, stirring occasionally.

WHITE SAUCE

Serves 4

Ingredients	Metric	Imperial	American
Butter or margarine	*25 g*	*1 oz*	*2 tbsp*
Plain flour	*25 g*	*1 oz*	*2 tbsp*
Milk	*300 ml*	*1/2 pt*	*1 1/4 cups*
Salt and pepper			

Put the butter or margarine in a bowl and microwave on High for 1 minute until melted. Work in the flour and gradually stir in the milk. Season with salt and pepper. Microwave on High for 6 minutes, stirring 3 times during cooking.

To Freeze: Freeze in a rigid container for up to 2 months.

To Serve: Microwave on High for 5-7 minutes, stirring frequently.

Cheese sauce – After cooking, stir in 50 g/2 oz/ 1/3 cup grated cheese.

Egg sauce – After cooking, stir in 2 finely chopped hard-boiled eggs.

Onion sauce – After cooking, stir in 2 finely chopped onions cooked in butter until soft and golden.

Parsley sauce – After cooking, stir in 30 ml/2 tablespoons chopped fresh parsley.

Mushroom sauce – After cooking, stir in 50 g/2 oz/ 1/2 cup finely chopped cooked mushrooms.

BREAD SAUCE

Serves 4

Ingredients	Metric	Imperial	American
Onion	*1*	*1*	*1*
Cloves	*6*	*6*	*6*
Milk	*300 ml*	*¹/₂ pt*	*1 ¹/₄ cups*
Fresh white			
breadcrumbs	*75 g*	*3 oz*	*1 ¹/₂ cups*
Butter or margarine	*25 g*	*1 oz*	*2 tbsp*
Salt and pepper			
Single cream	*30 ml*	*2 tbsp*	*2 tbsp*

Peel the onion and keep it whole. Stick the cloves into the onion. Put into a bowl with the milk and microwave on High for 4 minutes. Remove and discard the onion. Stir the breadcrumbs and butter or margarine into the milk and microwave on High for 2 minutes. Season with salt and pepper and stir in the cream. Microwave on High for 30 seconds and serve hot with poultry or game.

To Freeze: Freeze in a rigid container without the cream for up to 2 months.

To Serve: Reheat on High for 5 minutes, stirring frequently.

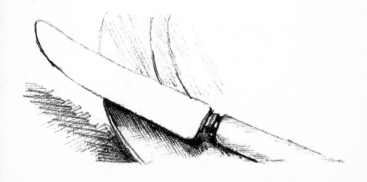

CURRY SAUCE

Serves 4

Ingredients	Metric	Imperial	American
Oil	30 ml	2 tbsp	2 tbsp
Onion, finely chopped	1	1	1
Plain flour	15 ml	1 tbsp	1 tbsp
Curry powder	30-	2-	2-
	45 ml	3 tbsp	3 tbsp
Curry paste	5 ml	1 tsp	1 tsp
Beef or chicken stock	450 ml	3/4 pt	2 cups
Eating apple	1	1	1
Sultanas (white			
raisins)	50 g	2 oz	1/3 cup
Lemon juice	10 ml	2 tsp	2 tsp
Salt and pepper			
Pinch of caster sugar			

Put the oil in a bowl and microwave on High for 30 seconds. Add the onion and microwave on High for 4 minutes, stirring once during cooking. Stir in the flour and curry powder and paste, mixing well, and then the stock. Peel and chop the apple and add to the bowl with the remaining ingredients. Cook in the microwave for 8 minutes, stirring twice during cooking. Serve with meat, poultry, vegetables, seafood or eggs.

COLESLAW DRESSING

Serves 4

Ingredients	Metric	Imperial	American
Sugar	50 g	2 oz	1/4 cup
White wine vinegar	150 ml	6 fl oz	3/4 cup
Water	120 ml	4 fl oz	1/2 cup
Celery seed	2.5 ml	1/2 tsp	1/2 tsp
Salt and pepper			

Put the cabbage, carrots, green pepper and onion into a large bowl. Sprinkle with salt and leave to stand for 1 hour. Drain.

Put all the ingredients into a casserole and microwave on High for 5-6 minutes until boiling, stirring several times. Continue to boil for 1 minute. Cool slightly.

To make the coleslaw mix 450 g/1 lb shredded white cabbage, 2 grated carrots, 1 grated apple, 1 chopped green pepper and 1 chopped onion. Pour over the coleslaw dressing and toss well.

To Freeze: Freeze the dressing in rigid containers for up to 2 weeks.

To Serve: Transfer the dressing from one container to a casserole dish and microwave on Medium for 5-6 minutes until defrosted, but still very cold, stirring once or twice. Leave to stand for 5-10 minutes.

CHOCOLATE SAUCE

Serves 4

Ingredients	Metric	Imperial	American
Water	*150 ml*	*$1/_4$ pt*	*$2/_3$ cup*
Caster sugar	*100 g*	*4 oz*	*$1/_2$ cup*
Cocoa powder	*50 g*	*2 oz*	*$1/_4$ cup*

Put the water into a jug and microwave on High for 3 minutes. Stir in the sugar until dissolved. Microwave on High for 2 minutes. Whisk in the cocoa powder and microwave on High for 1 minute. As the sauce cools and thickens, stir occasionally. Serve hot or cold over ices and puddings.

To Freeze: Freeze in a rigid container for up to 2 months.

To Serve: Reheat on High for 5 minutes, stirring occasionally.

APPLE SAUCE

Serves 4

Ingredients	Metric	Imperial	American
Cooking apples	*450 g*	*1 lb*	*1 lb*
Water	*30 ml*	*2 tbsp*	*2 tbsp*
Sugar	*50 g*	*2 oz*	*1/4 cup*
Butter or margarine	*25 g*	*1 oz*	*2 tbsp*

Peel and core the apples and cut them into thin slices. Put into a bowl with the other ingredients. Microwave on High for 3 minutes, stirring twice during cooking. Purée in a food processor or rub through a sieve until smooth. Reheat on High for 30 seconds and serve hot with pork or duck.

To Freeze: Freeze in a rigid container for up to 2 months.

To Serve: Reheat on High for 5 minutes, stirring occasionally.

BUTTERSCOTCH SAUCE

Serves 4

Ingredients	Metric	Imperial	American
Single cream	*150 ml*	*¼ pt*	*⅔ cup*
Dark soft brown sugar	*225 g*	*8 oz*	*1 cup*
Butter or margarine	*40 g*	*1 ½ oz*	*3 tbsp*
Few drops of vanilla essence (extract)			

Stir the cream, sugar and butter together in a bowl. Microwave on High for 4 minutes, stirring twice during cooking. Stir in the vanilla essence. Serve with ices or puddings.

To Freeze: Freeze in a rigid container for up to 2 months.

To Serve: Reheat on High for 5 minutes.

LEMON BUTTER

Serves 4

Ingredients	Metric	Imperial	American
Butter or margarine	*100 g*	*4 oz*	*½ cup*
Lemon juice	*15 ml*	*1 tbsp*	*1 tbsp*
Black pepper			

Cut the butter into small pieces and put in a bowl with the lemon juice and pepper. Microwave on High for 1 ½ minutes. Stir well and serve with fish or vegetables.

To Freeze: Freeze in a rigid container for up to 2 months.

To Serve: Reheat on High for 2 minutes.

INDEX